Wonders of Nature
Volcanoes

Dana Meachen Rau

Marshall Cavendish
Benchmark
New York

The ground shakes. A grey cloud forms over the top of the mountain. People leave as fast as they can. It is not safe to be near a volcano when it *erupts*!

The world's biggest volcano is Mauna Loa. It is Earth's largest mountain, but not the tallest. It covers half of the island of Hawaii.

Some volcanoes are shaped like tall mountains. Some are flat cracks on the ground.

There are even volcanoes at
the bottom of the ocean.

It is very hot deep inside the earth. It is so hot that rock melts. This melted rock is called *magma*.

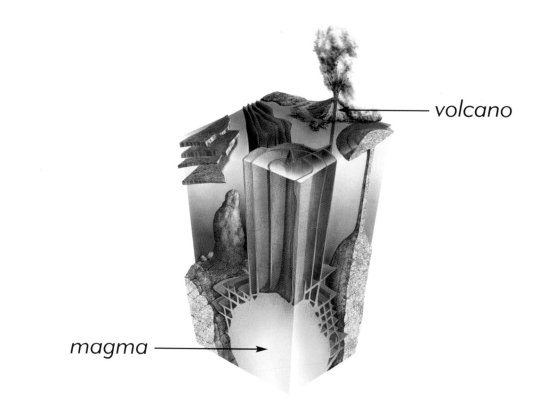

volcano

magma

The magma collects in a space inside the earth. Then it may travel up tunnels called _vents_.

The magma shoots out of
holes at the top or sides
of the volcano.

When magma comes out of a
volcano, it is called *lava*. Some
lava is slow and thick. People
can get close enough to study it.

Fast, thin lava quickly burns everything in its path.

Air helps cool the lava. If lava flows to the ocean, the water cools it, too. Lava gets hard when it cools. The lava turns back into rock.

Gases also erupt from a volcano. A volcano with a lot of gas erupts high into the sky. These gases make it hard for people to breathe.

Rocks also shoot out of volcanoes. Big ones are called volcanic bombs.

Smaller rocks shoot out, too.
The rocks fall from the sky
like rain.

Volcanoes also send *ash* into the air. Ash is like dust. It can travel hundreds of miles from a volcano. It covers houses, trees, and roads. It can even block out sunlight.

Ash once covered a whole town. Mount Vesuvius in Italy erupted almost two thousand years ago. Its ash buried all of the buildings and people in the town below.

Volcanoes change the land.
A volcano dumps ash, rock,
and lava around it. This makes
the land higher.

It might make a hole in the ground called a *crater*.

Not all volcanoes erupt. Some volcanoes have not erupted in a very long time. Some may never erupt again. They are still called volcanoes.

27

People want to know more about volcanoes. They study them to know when they might erupt. Then they can get others out of the way to a safe place.

Challenge Words

ash (ASH)—Tiny pieces of burnt rock.

crater (KRAYT-uhr)—A wide hole in the ground.

erupts (ee-RUPTS)—Bursts up from the ground.

gases (GAS-es)—Materials in the air that cannot be seen.

lava (LA-vuh)—Hot, melted rock that has erupted from a volcano.

magma (MAG-muh)—Hot, melted rock inside the earth.

vents (VENTS)—Openings for air, steam, or other gases to pass through.

Index

Page numbers in **boldface** are illustrations.

With thanks to Nanci Vargus, Ed.D.,
and Beth Walker Gambro, reading consultants

Marshall Cavendish Benchmark
99 White Plains Road
Tarrytown, New York 10591-9001
www.marshallcavendish.us

Library of Congress Cataloging-in-Publication Data

Rau, Dana Meachen, 1971–
Volcanoes / by Dana Meachen Rau.
p. cm. — (Bookworms. Wonders of nature)
Summary: "Provides a basic introduction to volcanoes, including geographical information
and what happens when they erupt"—Provided by publisher.
Includes index.
ISBN 978-0-7614-2670-7
1. Volcanoes—Juvenile literature. I. Title. II. Series.
QE521.3.R38 2007
551.21—dc22
2006038621

Editor: Christina Gardeski
Publisher: Michelle Bisson
Designer: Virginia Pope
Art Director: Anahid Hamparian

Photo Research by Anne Burns Images

Cover Photo by *Peter Arnold*/Helga Lade/GmbH, Germany

The photographs in this book are used with permission and through the courtesy of:
Peter Arnold: pp. 1, 6 BIOS; p. 7 Kelvin Aitken. *Corbis*: p. 2 Gary Braasch; p. 12 Corbis; p. 13 Roger Ressmeyer;
p. 15 Brenda Tharp; p. 16 epa; p. 22 Seamas Culligan/ZUMA; p.25 Mark. A. Johnson. *Photo Researchers*:
p. 5 NASA; p. 8 Stephen & Donna O'Meara; p. 10 Gary Hincks; p. 27 George Ranalli; p. 28 John Cole.
NOAA: pp. 11, 18, 19, 24. *AP Wide World Photos*: p. 21.

Printed in Malaysia
1 3 5 6 4 2